W9-CLS-354

DINOSAURS
WALKED HERE

DINOSAURS
WALKED HERE

and Other Stories Fossils Tell

by Patricia Lauber

ST. GABRIEL SCHOOL LIBRARY
MENTOR, OHIO

Macmillan/McGraw-Hill School Publishing Company
New York Chicago Columbus

ACKNOWLEDGMENTS

The author wishes to express her appreciation to Dr. Donald Baird, Director of the Museum of Natural History at Princeton University, for his more than generous help as expert reader of the manuscript, photographer, and willing provider of much useful information.

The author would also like to thank the individuals and institutions whose kind cooperation made possible the inclusion of a number of extraordinary illustrations.

ILLUSTRATION CREDITS

Donald Baird, pp. 2, 3, 4, 5 (right), 6, 8, 25, 26, 37, 42, 43, 46; Black Hills Institute of Geological Research, photo by Robert R. Reisz, p. 47; Edwin H. Colbert, p. 49 (left); W. P. Coombs, courtesy Dinosaur State Park, Connecticut, p. 34; Philip Currie/Tyrrell Museum of Palaeontology, p. 35; Field Museum of Natural History, Chicago, p. 11, Field Museum of Natural History and the artist, Charles R. Knight, pp. 14, 27; Doug Henderson, artist, in cooperation with John Horner and the Museum of the Rockies at Bozeman, Montana, pp. 36, 39; Doug Henderson in cooperation with John Horner, the Museum of the Rockies, and the Academy of Natural Sciences in Philadelphia, pp. 41, 52; John Horner, Museum of the Rockies, p. 38; Martin Lockley, pp. 32, 33; NASA, p. 44; George C. Page Museum, Los Angeles County Museum of Natural History, pp. 17, 19; George O. Poinar, Jr., Berkeley Amber Laboratory, p. 12; Smithsonian Institution, Photo No. 85-6814, p. 5 (left), No. 77-8474, p. 15, No. 77-7327, p. 18, pp. 28, 30; United States Department of the Interior, National Park Service, photo by Terry Maze, pp. 9, 10, 20, 23.

Cover: (top) *Edmontosaurus*, a duck-billed dinosaur (courtesy Smithsonian Institution); (left) a gnat in amber (courtesy George O. Poinar, Jr., Berkeley Amber Laboratory); (right) a fossil horseshoe crab (courtesy Donald Baird).

Frontispiece: Two *Grallator* footprints. (W. P. Coombs, courtesy Pratt Museum, Amherst College).

Half-title page: Fossil of a starfish that lived 450 million years ago. (courtesy Smithsonian Institution, Photo No. 13. Fs).

Chapter one opening: (Top) *Triceratops* (courtesy Smithsonian Institution, Photo No. 77-7777); (bottom) *Stegosaurus* (courtesy Smithsonian Institution, Photo No. 77-8094).

The text of this book is set in 14 pt. Caledonia.

Book design by Sylvia Frezzolini

Copyright © 1987 by Patricia Lauber

All rights reserved.

No part of this book may be reproduced or transmitted in any form or by any means, electronic or mechanical, including photocopying, recording or by any information storage and retrieval system, without permission in writing from the Publisher.

Bradbury Press, An Affiliate of Macmillan, Inc., 866 Third Avenue, New York, NY 10022. Collier Macmillan Canada, Inc.

For information regarding permission, write to Bradbury Press,
Macmillan Publishing Company, 866 Third Avenue, New York, NY 10022.
This edition is reprinted by arrangement with **Macmillan Publishing Company.**

Macmillan/McGraw-Hill School Division, 10 Union Square East, New York, New York 10003

Printed and bound in Mexico.
ISBN 0-02-274945-4

5 6 7 8 9 REY 99 98 97 96 95

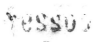

Contents

002297

DINOSAURS
WALKED HERE

The horned dinosaur *Triceratops* (top) seems to have been one of the last kinds to disappear from the earth. *Stegosaurus* (below) was an armored dinosaur, with spikes on its tail. The fossils of these and other dinosaurs tell us of the many kinds that roamed the earth tens of millions of years ago.

ONE

A Diary of the Past

Once there were dinosaurs. They roamed the earth for 140 million years but died out long before there were people to see them, tell of them, or draw their pictures. Even so, we know about them because we have found their bones, teeth, skin imprints, and footprints preserved in rock. These remains and traces of dinosaurs are called fossils. The same name is used for the remains and traces of all animals and plants that lived on earth long ago.

Fossils can be shells and bones. They can be prints of leaves and feathers. They can be eggs and insects, or the tracks of worms, birds, and dinosaurs. Whatever they may be, fossils are old. They are anywhere from thousands of years old to hundreds of millions of years old. Together they are like a diary that tells of the earth's past. They tell about plants and animals of long, long ago, about kinds that have died out, kinds that are still seen today, and kinds that developed into the plants and animals we know. They tell whether the earth was warmer or cooler than it is today. They tell of great changes in the surface of the earth—of continents that moved, of shallow seas that sparkled where now there are mountains or plains.

The story fossils tell is not complete because the earth's diary has many missing pages. Some were destroyed by changes in the earth. Some have not been found. Still other pages are blank. These were never written on because most living things do not become fossils when they die. Instead, they slowly disappear. Their soft parts decay as bacteria and other tiny forms of life feed on them. Their hard parts weather away, as wind and water wear them down. After a while, no trace of the plant or animal is left.

These are the footprints of a snipe-like shorebird that lived among the dinosaurs about 100 million years ago. No bones of this bird are known.

The fossil record shows that with the passing of time, many kinds of life, such as dinosaurs, died out. It shows that some kinds have lived on for millions of years and hardly changed at all.

One of these is the horseshoe crab, which today looks like a fossil relative that lived 140 million years ago.

Beavers still look like their fossil relatives, but are much smaller. Compare the skull of a modern beaver (left) with that of a bear-sized beaver that built huge beaver dams about 15,000 years ago.

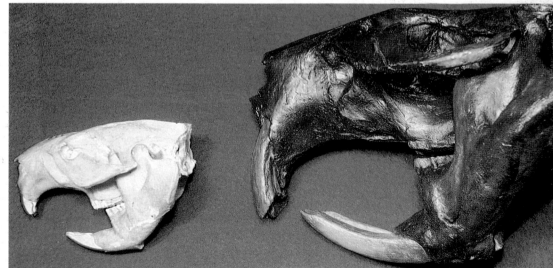

The fossil record also shows how some kinds of life developed. This 315-million-year-old amphibian (left) was the ancestor of today's salamanders . . .

and bullfrogs.

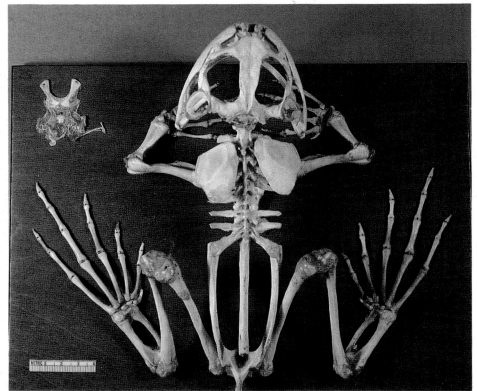

Archaeopteryx, the oldest known bird, lived about 140 million years ago. You can see the imprint of its long feathers in the limestone rock. It is thought to have been the ancestor of . . .

modern birds, such as this barn owl.

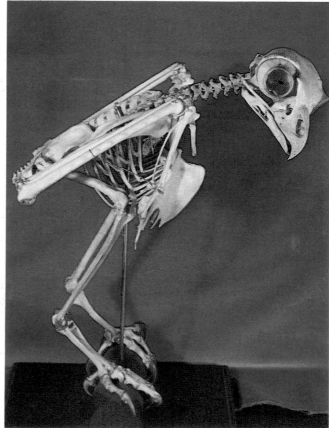

Yet sometimes this does not happen. Suppose a fish dies and settles to the bottom of a lake. The bottom is covered with soft sediments—sand, clay, silt, mud, or other fine materials. The fish's body sinks into the sediments. A current sweeps sand over the fish and buries it. Still other sediments settle out of the water on top of the fish.

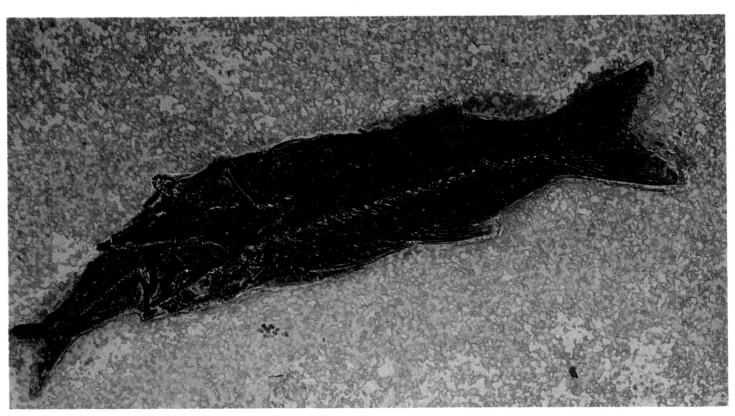

About 50 million years ago, near what is now Fossil, Wyoming, two fishes died as the larger tried to swallow the smaller.

The soft parts of the fish soon decay. But the bones are left, buried in sediment. As the years go by, more and more layers of sediment pile up on top of the bones. The new layers press down on the old ones. Water may add minerals that act like glue, cementing the sediments together. Over many, many years the old sediments harden into rock. Inside the rock is a fossil—the bones of the fish.

Rock that forms in this way is called sedimentary rock, because it is made of hardened sediments. Three common sedimentary rocks are shale, sandstone, and limestone. Shale is made mostly of clay. Sandstone, as the name tells you, is made mostly of sand. Limestone may form from chemicals that settle out of water, or it may form from the shells of sea animals.

Most sediments come from other rocks. Tiny bits of rock are worn away by wind and rain and frost. They are washed into streams that flow into rivers. The rivers flow into lakes or seas. When water is moving, it carries sediments along. When it slows, sediments settle out of it. That is why most fossils are the remains of plants or animals that died where there was water—seas, lakes, streams, swamps, or floodplains, which are flat areas that sometimes flood. Here they were most likely to be quickly buried in sediments and preserved in rock.

There are other ways in which fossils form. Plants and animals can, for example, be buried by wind-blown sand or by the ash and mudflows of erupting volcanoes. But most are found in the layers of rock that formed from sediments carried by water.

Often changes take place in the parts of plants and animals buried in

Long, long ago a river flowed across this now dry land in Montana. Sand settled out of its waters and built up in its channels. In time the sand became the sedimentary rock called sandstone. Still later the river dried up. Rain, frost, and wind wore away the riverbanks, exposing the sandstone. Today they wear away the sandstone, exposing fossils. Scientists, on their hands and knees, are picking up the fossil teeth and bones of animals that lived some 60 million years ago.

sediment. In one type of change, water trickles into bones. It fills all the tiny spaces in the bones, just as water fills the holes in a sponge. The water carries minerals that settle out. Over a long period of time the tiny spaces become filled with solid minerals. The bones are now much harder than before. They have become petrified, which means "turned to stone."

The same thing may happen with parts of plants. Petrified wood is wood that became filled with minerals while it was buried under layers of sediment.

Some 200 million years ago, huge trees were uprooted and carried miles away by an ancient river. Where they came to rest they were buried under sediments. Today the sedimentary rock has weathered away, exposing the petrified wood, which forms Petrified Forest National Park, in Arizona.

This polished slice of a petrified tree trunk gleams with colored minerals that settled out of water.

A different kind of change may take place with a shelled animal, such as a clam. The soft body of the clam decays. The shell becomes a fossil. But after a great deal of time has passed, water may dissolve the shell. The shell disappears but leaves its imprint in the hardened rock. The imprint is a fossil. Perhaps the shell has also filled with minerals that harden. When the shell dissolves, it leaves its inside shape imprinted in those minerals. The shape is also a fossil.

In the same way, fossil leaves may break down, but their imprint remains in the hardened rock. Sometimes the imprint is black or brown, a mark of the carbon that was in the leaf.

Some fossils are not parts of animals but traces of things animals did. These fossils may be footprints or other tracks, burrows, signs of feeding, or other clues to how animals lived.

Seed fern lived some 300 million years ago.

Once in a great while people find fossils that formed in still other ways. Some of these are whole animals that were preserved for tens of thousands of years or even millions of years.

Forty-million-year-old gnat is embedded in amber. Green is caused by the breaking up of white light as it passes through tiny cracks in the amber.

TWO

Gnats, Mammoths, and Saber-toothed Tigers

One day, forty million years ago, a gnat was crawling over the bark of a pine tree. It became trapped in a sticky flow of sap, or resin. Once the gnat was covered with resin, no other animal could eat it. The soft parts of the body did not decay, because bacteria could not feed on them. The gnat was quickly preserved. Much later, the resin hardened into the kind of fossil called amber, which looks something like yellow glass. Inside the amber was another fossil, the gnat. The gnat is one of many fossil insects that have been found in amber.

Quick freezing preserved the bodies of some woolly mammoths. Mammoths were relatives of today's elephants. They were able to live through a time of great changes in the earth's climate—through an ice age. They lived through times when mile-thick sheets of ice crept out from the polar regions and down from mountains to cover once-green lands. They lived through times when the ice melted and shrank back, releasing floods of meltwater. Then, when the ice last shrank back to the polar regions and mountaintops, about 9,000 to 12,000 years ago, the woolly mammoths died out, for reasons no one knows.

Woolly mammoths, shown in this painting, lived through times when huge sheets of ice covered large parts of the earth and times when the ice melted, releasing floods of water.

When the ice age ended, large mammals, such as mastodons (above) and mammoths, died out.

We know about woolly mammoths from the cave drawings of Stone Age people. We also know about them because whole frozen mammoths have been found in the ground of Alaska and Siberia. One of these was a baby mammoth that somehow lost its mother 27,000 years ago and fell into an icy pit, where it died. Bacteria had little chance to feed on the body because it soon froze and became covered with ice. The sides of the pit caved in and

ST. GABRIEL SCHOOL LIBRARY
MENTOR, OHIO

002297

buried the baby mammoth under six feet of earth. At that depth, the summer sun could not melt the ice or thaw the body. The body of the baby mammoth was preserved. It was discovered in 1977 by Soviet gold prospectors working in northeastern Siberia. The body was so well preserved that scientists could even find traces of its mother's milk in the mammoth's stomach.

The bones of animals have been found preserved in still another way. These are the bones of animals that were trapped in places where oil was oozing out of the ground as thick, sticky asphalt. One of these places is now known as the La Brea tar pits, in Los Angeles. Scientists suppose the animals were trapped in ways like this:

Thousands of years ago, a ground sloth the size of an elephant was being chased by a saber-toothed tiger. Lumbering across the valley as fast as it could, the sloth glimpsed a shining surface that looked like a pond. It plunged in, hoping to escape the tiger. The big saber-tooth sprang after it. But the water was only a thin layer that had collected on top of asphalt, and both animals were trapped in the sticky ooze. As they died, giant vultures dived from the sky to feed on them. One came too close to the surface, dragged its feet in the asphalt, and could not free itself.

At other times animals may have waded in to drink, only to discover they could not get out. Sometimes plant-eating animals may have scattered and fled from a meat eater. Some ran across what looked like solid ground, but an asphalt pool lay under the leaves or dirt. And so over the years many animals were trapped. Among them were camels, mammoths, bears, wolves, lions, bison, antelope, geese, and eagles. Long afterward their bones were

Giant vultures watch as a saber-toothed tiger threatens a giant ground sloth, in this painting of a La Brea tar pit.

The saber-toothed tiger is one of many animals, known from their fossils, that lived and flourished in North America and then died out for reasons no one knows.

discovered at La Brea, preserved as fossils in the asphalt. The bones told a story of animals that used to live in North America and of some that died out as mysteriously as the woolly mammoths.

Fossils tell much about plants and animals of the past. The study of fossils also tells of changes in the face of the earth and of changes in the earth's climate.

The giant ground sloth is another animal known only from its fossils.

Paleontologists work on
fossil bones at Dinosaur
National Monument,
in Utah.

THREE

Layers of Fossils

The study of fossils is called paleontology, which means "the study of ancient forms of life." Scientists who study fossils are paleontologists. Paleontologists are often the finders of fossils. But many times they first hear of a find from other people—from rock collectors who came upon fossils, from miners or construction workers who found fossils while digging. Amateur fossil hunters may report a find. Sometimes someone simply sees a bone sticking out of the ground. This happens because sedimentary rocks are fairly soft and crumbly. They are easily worn away by wind and water. Fossils long buried in the rock may then be exposed.

Some finds tell of great changes in the face of the earth. Climbers, for example, may come upon seashells in rocks near the tops of mountains. The fossil shells are a sign that the rocks formed from sediments at the bottom of an ancient sea. At a later time mountains crumpled up out of the earth's crust. The seabed and its fossils were carried skyward.

Fossils also tell of changes in climate. Today, for example, the northeastern part of Yellowstone National Park has rugged mountains and a climate that is cool in summer and very cold in winter. It has forests of firs and other evergreens that grow well in a cold climate. About fifty million years ago, it was very different. In place of the mountains there were broad, flat river valleys separated by rolling hills. The climate was mild in the hills and hot in the valleys.

We know about this change in climate because paleontologists have found forests of fossil trees in this part of the park. These were leafy trees that grow in mild to hot climates.

The forests were preserved because of huge volcanic eruptions that buried them in ash and rocks. After each big eruption, new forests took root on top of the old ones. Over many, many years, minerals from moving water turned the buried tree trunks to stone. Now, millions of years later, the volcanic material around the tree trunks has weathered away. The petrified remains of ancient trees can be seen standing upright exactly where the trees used to grow.

In one area, forests were buried many times. Wind, rain, and melting snow have worn away the side of a steep bluff, exposing more than twenty layers of petrified trees. They formed over some 20,000 years, as volcanic eruptions buried a forest, a new forest grew, and eruptions buried it. The result is like a giant layer cake. Each layer of forest—of tree trunks and imprints of leaves—tells its own story about plants and climate. Each is like a page in the earth's diary.

Fossil tree stumps and leaves found in Yellowstone National Park tell of a time, 50 million years ago, when the climate was mild and damp and the trees that grew were broad-leaved hardwoods.

Sedimentary rock also forms in layers. Each new layer marks a change in the sediments that were being laid down. A river, for example, might flow slowly for years, carrying along only very fine sediments and dropping them in a bay. Then a huge storm strikes upstream. Water pours into the river and the river's flow speeds up. The faster flow means that the water picks up coarse sediments as well as fine. Now it drops sand and gravel in the bay. Later the river goes back to carrying only fine sediments. The sand and gravel mark the end of one layer of fine sediment and the start of another.

You have probably seen such layers. They often appear where the sea has eaten away at a cliff or a river has carved a deep valley. They are seen where wind and rain have worn down hills and mountains. They are also seen in quarries and where road cuts pass through hills.

Paleontologists find the layers useful because they are like time capsules. Plants and animals that appear as fossils in the same layers must have lived at the same time. That is how paleontologists have learned about the world of the dinosaurs. They know what kinds of plants grew in that world. They

To lay railroad track in eastern Ohio, workers made a cut in a cliff, revealing rock layers laid down some 300 million years ago. At the bottom is limey mudstone that built up in the bed of a large lake. Within the mudstone are layers of limestone, holding fossil fishes. The lake grew shallow and became overgrown with plants, forming a peat bog. Much later the remains of the bog became coal (brown layer). Next a floodplain developed, with rivers and lakes. Layers of sandstone and mudstone were laid down. Coal-swamp plants took over again and their remains led to another layer of coal (black layer). The land sank slightly and a lake formed. It gradually filled with layers of limey mudstone or shale and limestone, which go to the top of the cliff.

know what the climate was like. They know what other kinds of animals shared that world. The layers, like the fossils themselves, fill out our picture of dinosaurs and how they lived.

If you look closely, you will see that this slice of rock has pairs of thin layers, one dark and one light. The sediments forming the dark layers were laid down in a lake during summer and fall. The light layers were laid down in winter and spring. The summer-fall layers are darker because the sediments were discolored by rotting leaves, dust, pollen, and soot from forest fires. Each pair stands for one year. The dark spots you see are fossils. The wide, light-colored bands occur about every hundred years. They mark a change in sediments that was probably caused by a change in climate.

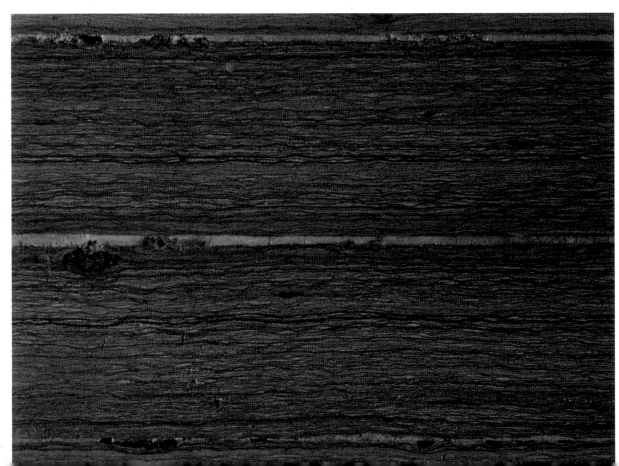

By studying fossils from the same layers of sedimentary rock, paleontologists can tell what kinds of plants and animals lived at the same time dinosaurs did.

Edmontosaurus was one of the duck-billed dinosaurs.

FOUR

Dinosaurs Walked Here

Using fossil bones, paleontologists can make skeletons of dinosaurs. The skeletons show what the animals looked like and how they moved about, whether they walked on two feet or on four.

Fossil teeth are clues to what dinosaurs ate. By studying teeth paleontologists have learned that most dinosaurs were plant eaters, but some ate animals. Duck-billed dinosaurs, for example, had hundreds of teeth in their jaws. The teeth in each jaw were pressed together and formed a rough plate. These teeth were suited to grinding up plants. *Tyrannosaurus rex* had teeth that were six inches long, with edges like saws. These teeth were suited to tearing through flesh.

Some dinosaurs even ate other dinosaurs. Skeletons of plant-eating dinosaurs sometimes have a meat eater's broken-off teeth stuck in their bones.

Fossil tracks and trails offer still more clues to how dinosaurs behaved.

The teeth of duckbills (above) were pressed together into rough plates suited to grinding up plant food. *Tyrannosaurus rex* (below) had teeth suited to tearing through flesh.

Most of these tracks formed when dinosaurs happened to walk across the kind of place where their footprints were likely to be preserved.

We have all left footprints in mud or sand, but most of these do not last. In mud they usually blur and disappear. In sand they are soon erased by wind or water. Yet from time to time you do see footprints that have dried and lasted.

You are most likely to find them in places that have been flooded. Here high waters have drawn back, leaving fine-grained sediments behind. Along the shores of seas this is likely to happen after the highest tide of the year. Inland it is likely to happen after a rainy season has raised a stream or pond to its highest level. Footprints made in these moist surfaces have a chance to harden after the waters draw back. Then they may be buried under sediments from later floods and preserved. That is how most fossil tracks of dinosaurs formed.

Studies of tracks show that many earlier ideas about dinosaurs were wrong. Scientists used to think that dinosaurs were slow-moving and even clumsy. They thought that brontosaurs and other giant plant eaters must have spent their lives in lakes, swamps, and other places where water helped to support their weight. Some scientists wondered whether these dinosaurs could walk on land at all. Paleontologists thought that meat-eating dinosaurs could not swim. They pictured plant eaters as browsing safely in lakes while hungry meat eaters stood on the shores. And because today's reptiles do not live in social groups, scientists long thought that dinosaurs also lived alone. Today all these ideas have changed.

These footprints were left by a camptosaur, a plant-eating dinosaur, on the shoreline of a 150-million-year-old lake in western Oklahoma.

Measurements of dinosaur tracks show that some kinds were quick and agile. They did not waddle along with their feet wide apart but walked mostly on their hind legs, in long strides, with their feet fairly close together. Some medium-sized meat eaters could travel as fast as a human runner can sprint, at about ten miles an hour. Plant-eating dinosaurs moved more slowly. Their top speed was about four miles an hour, which was also the speed of the slowest meat eaters.

Brontosaur tracks in Texas and other states show that these giant plant eaters could and did walk on land. In fact, they were good walkers, moving with long strides.

Two brontosaurs walked over very soft sediments along the shore of a 150-million-year-old lake in southeastern Colorado and left these tracks behind.

Tracks at Dinosaur State Park in Connecticut suggest that at least some meat eaters could swim. There, hundreds of footprints have been preserved in the sediments of an ancient lake. Most of the footprints were made by medium-sized meat-eating dinosaurs. One set shows unusually clear claw marks, a sign that the dinosaur was not putting any weight on its feet. It appears to have been swimming in shallow water and kicking the bottom with the tips of its toes.

Many tracks of meat-eating dinosaurs have been found at what is now Dinosaur State Park in Connecticut. One set shows unusually clear claw marks, which may mean the dinosaur was swimming in shallow water, kicking the bottom with its toes.

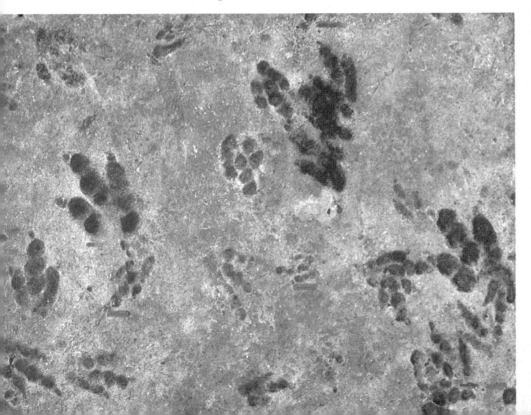

Studies of fossil tracks also show that some dinosaurs lived in herds, or social groups. In Texas there are tracks of twenty or more large, plant-eating dinosaurs walking abreast and moving in the same direction. In British Columbia there are tracks made by a large herd of duck-billed dinosaurs. The adults were spread out along a broad front, sometimes walking side by side. Young duckbills followed behind, often stepping on the adults' footprints.

Along the Peace River in British Columbia paleontologists found many tracks of plant-eating dinosaurs, which appear to have been moving in herds.

An artist, working with a paleontologist, drew this picture of young duckbills following an adult.

Tracks in British Columbia and Massachusetts show that some small- to medium-sized meat-eating dinosaurs hunted in packs. But big meat eaters seem to have hunted alone or in pairs. No tracks have been found of groups moving together. In Montana, other kinds of fossils also tell of dinosaurs that lived in groups. These fossils are eggs, eggshells, and young dinosaurs that lived some eighty million years ago.

At that time a broad, shallow sea ran north-south through the middle of North America. To the west of the sea were the newly formed Rocky Mountains and a few volcanoes. A wide coastal plain stretched from the Rockies to the inland sea. Rivers cut their way through the plain, dropping sediments from the mountains in swamps, marshes, and the sea. Fossils show the climate was wet and warm and plant life was like that of southern Louisiana today.

Many kinds of animals lived on the plain. Among them were duck-billed dinosaurs and horned dinosaurs, as well as meat-eating dinosaurs.

The dinosaur fossils presented a puzzle. There were many bones, but nearly all were the bones of adults. Why was there almost no sign of young dinosaurs or eggs?

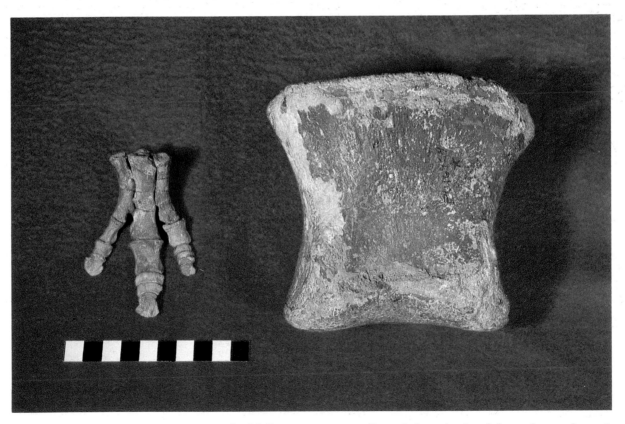

Compared with their parents, young duckbills were very small. At left is the hind foot of a nestling. At right is one toe bone from an adult. Black-and-white scale is 10 centimeters (4 inches) long.

The puzzle was solved when paleontologists discovered dinosaur nesting grounds. The dinosaurs had had special places where females laid their eggs. Here nests, eggs, broken eggshells, and the remains of young dinosaurs were found in several layers of sedimentary rock, a sign that the nesting grounds had been used over a long period of time.

Two of the nesting grounds are now small hills. In the days of dinosaurs one was an island in a lake and the other may have been a peninsula. The lake waters probably made the nesting grounds safe places to lay eggs.

Females of the same kind banded together in colonies to lay their eggs. One kind was the long-legged hypsilophodont. This fairly small dinosaur laid clutches of up to twenty-four eggs in a circular nest. Each nest was about

Hypsilophodonts laid clutches of up to 24 eggs.

Hypsilophodonts were long-legged and agile, as shown in this drawing.

six feet away from its nearest neighbors. The eggs had been laid in mud but were only partly covered by it. Paleontologists think that parents must have covered the eggs with parts of plants, the way female alligators do today. As the plants decay, they give off heat, which incubates the eggs.

Bones of young hypsilophodonts were found near the nests. Some of these young dinosaurs were newly hatched, but the bottoms of the eggs were neither crushed nor broken. This was a sign that the young left their nests after hatching out. If they had stayed in the nests, they would have broken the shells. Some of the young were older than others. This probably means that the young stayed in the nest area after hatching and found their food in the lake.

At least one other kind of dinosaur used the same nesting grounds. This one laid its eggs in paired rows. The eggs were covered with mud and needed the heat of the sun to incubate. No one is sure what kind of dinosaur this was.

About half a mile from these two nesting grounds, a third one was found. It was used by duckbills. These dinosaurs made big, bowl-shaped nests out of mud. Each nest was about six feet across and three feet deep. Like the nests of the hypsilophodonts, these were clustered together in a group. But they were littered with broken eggshells and some nests held the remains of young duck-billed dinosaurs.

Some paleontologists think that young duckbills were helpless when they hatched out, just as certain kinds of young birds are. They think the young stayed in their nests and were guarded and fed by their parents. This, they say, would account for the smashed eggshells and for the dead young, which may have starved when their parents failed to return with food. These scientists also point out that duck-billed dinosaurs of all ages were slow walkers. Young duckbills may have needed the protection of their parents, unlike young hypsilophodonts, which were speedy runners.

Duck-billed dinosaurs had nesting grounds where they made big bowl-shaped nests, as shown in this drawing.

This young duckbill died while hatching out of its egg.

Other paleontologists agree that at least some dinosaurs nested in groups and guarded their eggs. But they doubt that duck-billed dinosaurs fed their young because this is not something today's reptiles do.

Perhaps further digging will settle the question and tell more about these big dinosaurs that used to roam the earth, at a time when it looked very different than it does today.

This young duckbill was one of fifteen found together in an abandoned nest. An adult found nearby may have been the mother. Some paleontologists think the young starved to death after their mother died.

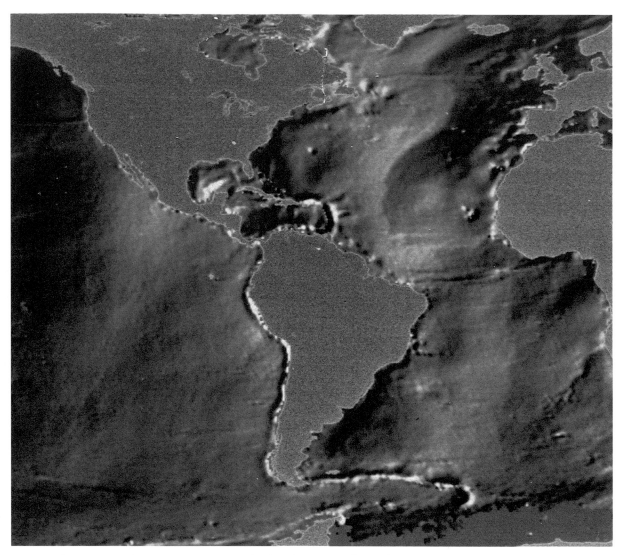

This satellite image shows the jigsaw-puzzle fit of Africa and South America.

FIVE

A Changing Earth

On a map Africa and South America look as if they could be fitted together, like pieces of a jigsaw puzzle. People first noticed this fit some four hundred years ago, after explorers mapped the coastlines of the continents. A few even wondered if the continents had somehow moved. But the idea seemed so unlikely that no one gave it much thought for the next three hundred years.

Then the idea came up again. It came up because scientists started discovering fossils that were hard to explain, unless whole continents had moved.

About 300 million years ago, for example, there were many of the large-leafed plants called *Glossopteris*. Their fossils have been found in South America, South Africa, Australia, India, and Antarctica, places that are thousands of miles apart and have very different climates. Had exactly the same plants developed in all these places? This did not seem likely to scientists.

The fossil remains of *Glossopteris* have been found in places that today are thousands of miles apart and have very different climates.

Or had the plants developed on a single continent that later broke up? To many scientists that seemed a more likely explanation of the fossils. But no one could explain how a continent might split up or how the pieces might move.

At about that same time in the earth's history there was a small reptile called *Mesosaurus*, which lived in fresh or slightly salty water. Its fossils were found in only two places: the east coast of Brazil and the west coast of South Africa. It did not seem likely that *Mesosaurus* could have crossed the Atlantic Ocean by swimming. How could the fossils be explained unless the two continents had once been joined?

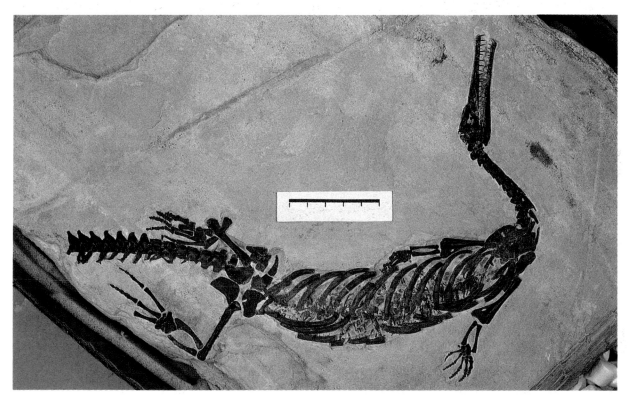

Fossils of *Mesosaurus* were found only on the east coast of Brazil and the west coast of Africa. *Mesosaurus* grew to a length of about two feet.

Fossils also showed that Antarctica was once a warm, wet land. It has fossils of *Glossopteris*. Fossil wood tells of forests that grew near what is now the South Pole. Antarctica also has beds of coal, which formed from plants that grew in tropical forests. These facts were hard to explain if Antarctica had always been at the South Pole.

One scientist working in Antarctica found a fossil jawbone from a group of animals called labyrinthodonts that lived two hundred million years ago. Labyrinthodonts were about the size of alligators and spent part of their time on land and part in fresh water—they were amphibians. Other fossils show that labyrinthodonts also lived in Africa, South America, and Australia. How had they reached Antarctica? Today's amphibians cannot live in salt water, and scientists doubt that ancient ones could either. Again, scientists wondered if Antarctica had moved.

Fossils and many other clues all seemed to say that continents had moved around in the past. They seemed to say that continents had collided and moved apart several times in the history of the earth. But it was not until the 1960s that earth scientists began to discover how such great changes might take place.

Earth scientists now think that the earth's rocky shell is made up of a number of huge slabs, or plates. The plates float on thick, hot, molten rock inside the earth, and they are in motion. As the plates move, they carry along whatever is on top of them—the ocean floor, islands, and whole continents. The plates move slowly, perhaps an inch or two a year. But over millions and millions of years, the inches add up to long distances.

This labyrinthodont was found on the south shore of the Ross Sea in Antarctica, about 300 miles from the South Pole. It is between 245 and 250 million years old. In life it had a long body and a long tail. The letters on the skull were placed there by a paleontologist. They are abbreviations of the scientific names of the bones.

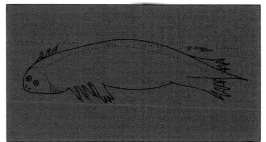

About three hundred million years ago, earth scientists say, all the earth's continents collided. They formed one supercontinent, which was surrounded by one giant ocean. On this huge continent many kinds of plants and animals developed, lived, and spread. Then molten rock welled up from inside the earth. As it spread outward, it tore the giant continent in two. Later the two big continents were torn into smaller pieces. These moved away from one another on plates, carrying their animals and plants. In time the pieces became the continents we know. The spaces between them became the oceans of today.

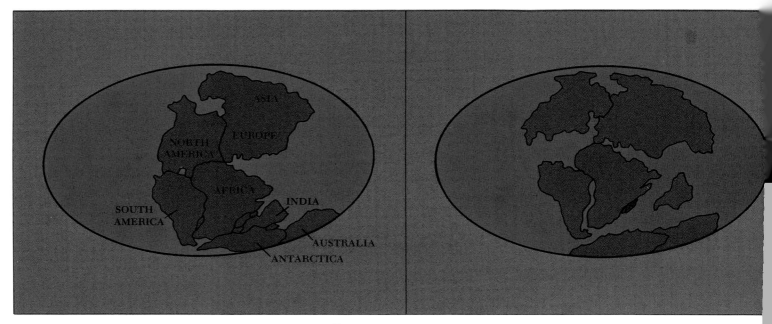

Earth scientists think that about 300 million years ago all the land masses collided and formed one giant continent.

Later this supercontinent split in two and then into smaller pieces.

ST. GABRIEL SCHOOL LIBRARY
MENTOR, OHIO

Fossils were among the clues that led to the discovery that continents move. Scientists still use them to figure out where continents have been and what changes have taken place. They find, for example, that the Americas collided with Africa and later separated again. But when the continents tore apart, a piece of western Africa traveled away with the Americas. Today we call this piece Florida. Fossils and rock found in Florida match fossils and rock from western Africa. They are very different from the rock and fossils found just to the north of Florida, in Georgia.

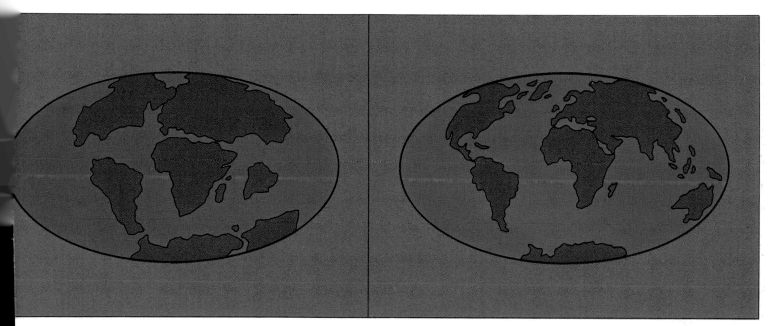

These pieces became the continents we know today.

002297

Like entries in a diary, fossils tell of the earth's history. They tell of continents that move, of changes in the face of the earth, of past climates. They tell of many kinds of past life, including the dinosaurs that walked here long ago.

Index